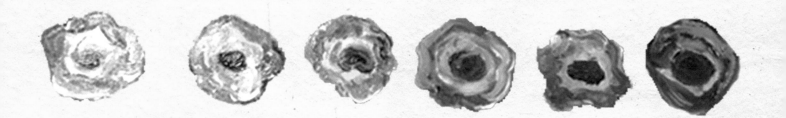

Jason's Pause

(Jason: Greek origin, meaning healer)

Elizabeth Clayton

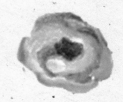

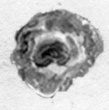

AuthorHouse™
1663 Liberty Drive
Bloomington, IN 47403
www.authorhouse.com
Phone: 1 (800) 839-8640

All paintings and sculptures pictured in the book are works of Elizabeth Clayton.

Image credit: One large image of a painting done by Elizabeth placed in the back of the book, was based off of the painting: A Medieval Flower Garden by Jenny de Gex, Great Britain, 1995

This book was assisted throughout by Tonia Germany and Judith Shearer

Published by AuthorHouse 08/13/2019

ISBN: 978-1-7283-1413-6 (sc)
ISBN: 978-1-7283-1414-3 (e)

Library of Congress Control Number: 2019942729

Print information available on the last page.

This book is printed on acid-free paper.

authorHOUSE®

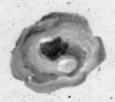

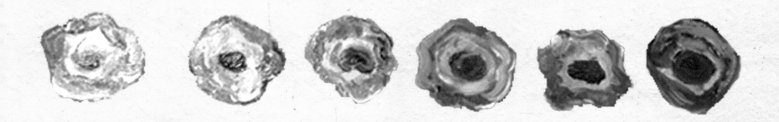

Contents

Preface vii

The verses: enlarging fable and truth 1

Conclusion..75

Elizabeth Afterthought 76

A Worded Rose 77

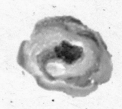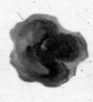

  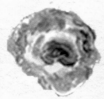   

Upright, stalwart –
judiciously tender
in love;
Observant of the all good,
Elusive, ever, of the enduring
Noblesse of truth –
Bless mon Coeur
–bedded Rosemary, for your thoughts
to lie within –

  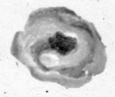  

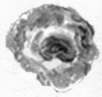

Preface

(Including Introductory Remarks)

When an artist/writer wishes to effect a work without error, such probably will not occur – like so, these verses behind, were composed some years ago, amid a time of much loss and hours of reflection. I, then, do confuse sentiment and vocabulary, omitting details and specifics, but the theme, the purposed wisdom, remains strong.

I must acknowledge my long-time assistant and friend, Tonia Germany, for her excellent work, as always, getting the manuscript, in good form, to press, especially, the fine color work. And I do believe we let "slip" by several verses that have already been included in other works – but, as I have stated, the theme, remains strong, a beautiful wisdom to add to living fully, honorably, in the all good.

"Jason" is my second eldest nephew, first of two sons to my youngest "frère" but more, my dear and knowing, giving, friend, my insightfully appreciative comrade with whom beauty, in its true, is our bond. Noble, kingly words – and kingship has always been a difficult matter. It provides for actions noble and those not so noble. When a male child was born to kingship – or, more, in olden times – he was, regardless of personal qualities, born into the tutelage of men often able, loyal to their kingdom and court. Tutors and all manner of well-prepared mentors and schooled companions were provided, certainly in the encompassment of the church, and, if not as much, more to guide the state.

Many of these young men did not come to the crown, but their lessons were with them throughout their preparation for life, often in great magnitude; prayer desks, candles, manuscripts, vestments and many such pieces remain as precious memorabilia, today – also, a courage and strength, alongside the corrupt and tawdry, as circumstances allowed. Until recent times, too little was ever spoken of lineage, tradition or royalty's place beside the Divine.

King Charles I was beheaded on January 1, 1630, the result of ridiculous charges of treason. The day was cold, and the king asked his valet for two extra sweaters to wear under his coat, so as not to appear to be trembling from fear, walking to his beheading before his people. And so he did. Noblesse is a royal trait, not hypocritical, but taught to be certain, true – this – the given trait to the white hart, to be hunted only by royalty.

Of our two worlds – that inner and outer – we learn through sounds, shapes, colors, fragrances, and different arrangements of these entities – but there is imbued in each of us – no matter the unknown particulars – our very own physical and spiritual manner of the arrangement; and the resulting reality is ours alone, beautiful,

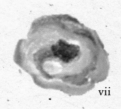

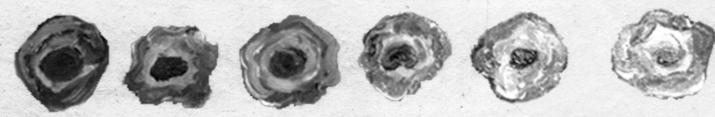

in the particulars, for these factors are as haloes, echoes, rainbows, breath, and fragrance – these poured out in The Divine pleasure of our I-Thou relationship.

We do not know, nor can we understand, the all answers, but the world is, and always has been, (regardless of the unnumbered thoughts of "Why") – beautiful, powerful, grand: "... the very face of God." (Kingsley) A season is a flower of different colors and shapes, fragrances; the time as such is measured by the sun and the sun's turns to its purposed center. A second glance to a flower in its second turn is good, for it speaks, in simplicity, of the complex great of The Ultimate I-Thou relationship.

"Hart," is an archaic word for "stag," (DE HEOROT - deer hall as in "Beowulf") – there was the Dutch hart, and the French hart was known in Medieval times also; these deer were described as red deer stags, more than five years of age. Such was a beast of "venery," the most prestigious form of hunting, very much above the fox – the hart, "Red Deer," was first in all classes, being sought out by hounds toward unknown scent, and continued on the hot scent.

A white stag (hind – female) is a white- colored, red or fallow deer resulting from a condition known as Laicism that causes its hair and skin to lose its natural color. Such is a rare genetic pattern, and ranges from hair color of red to brown, but not albino – there are no red eyes caused by a reduced pigmentation in all skin, not just melanin.

In reviewing mythology, as well as ancient histories, many interesting animals have been described – some from truth, and others with added fable. Indeed, many reflect the secret needs of the peoples from whom they come. Whether the white color is real or fable, the animal serves those who enjoy knowing his story well.

The color, white, is at its most complete, and pure, the color of perfection. There is much to be said, and much written of the color white, and magical, fanciful, other worldly activity. Fables and legends abound as deeply into history as spoken and written words. And representations in fine arts are found. In the ancient culture of China mythology is described the "Galan," the Chinese unicorn, shown in clay with a variety of "horns" that represent a unicorn, or, perhaps, a white hart. Being one of the oldest cultures, the white (red) ox alongside the Native Americans' white hart (deer) was a prominent creature in Europe during the Medieval period.

The ox in Chinese mythology is recorded in early sources as that of the Qulin people who were red-haired and had white faces, claiming to be decedents of a mating of a cow and a god in a mountain cave. In the Chinese zodiac the ox ranks second in zodiac symbols as being an animal of diligence, charity, honesty, patience and ambition. The Ming Dynasty continued the metamorphosing of the white face and red hair. The color of white has long been associated with purity, and in the Celtic culture also represented the otherworld. For early man, the deer represented valuable resources, providing food, clothing, and other accessories.

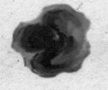

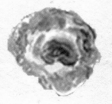

In Christianity, legend held the white stag as partly responsible for the conversion of martyr saints Eustace and Hubert. But perhaps most familiarity is with the first line of Psalm 42 (KJ Authorized Version), (1604-1611), "As the hart panteth after the water brook, so panteth my soul after Thee, Oh, God."

The white hart's reputation improved in the period of the Arthurian legends, where its appearance was a sign to Arthur and his knights to undertake a new quest. It was considered the one animal which could never be captured, coming to symbolize humanity's never-ending pursuance of knowledge and the unattainable. It came then, in a short period that Christianity managed to appropriate the white hart for its own purposes: the white stag came to symbolize Christ – His Presence on earth.

Legends are often born when we are able to find beauty, purity, and personal awareness, if yet the source is elusive. The color white offers purity, innocence, and suggests goodness with truth and the white hart was the badge of King Richard II of England, probably derived from the arms of his mother, Joan, "the fair maid of Kent," heiress of Edmund of Woodstock. This arrangement might have been a pun on his name, "Rich-hart." Rich with hart is recumbent and wears a gold crown as a collar, attached to a gold crown symbolizing both the suffering of Christ and Richard's burden of kingship, both noble and enslaved.

Pity is associated with his rule and asserted divine authority; the emblem features prominently as a notable piece of Fourteenth Century religious art. Richard is shown in the painting as wearing a gold and enameled white hart jewel, and even the angels surrounding the Virgin Mary all wear white hart badges – a white hart is shown on a bed of rosemary, symbolizing remembrance and sorrow.

The pastoral theme is old, in all of literature, approaching the years immediately before the Industrial Revolution, beside the publication of <u>The Origin of the Species</u>; The Medieval Period finished its thousand years, trade and commerce with the East (a result of religious fervor and trade spreading throughout the known world) came to be the norm; it grew quickly into a traumatic time with a new theory of man's existence – he, being the center of the universe, not God, who had been in the dominant position. Cities, factories, travel, a strong "push" to relieve man's physical burdens onto helping tools, machines and such came to be an accepted way of life.

The pastoral theme offered figures that became the death of the natural, such as mechanization increasing. Today, these figures (hart, unicorn, and such) are more celebratory as unusual than related to spirit. In the early existence of man, life was beautiful and difficult. Its beauty lay in absolute being: leaves and trees, into skies of blue and soft white; winds were, most, temperate and often fragrant, and flowers, berries, plums, melons and other varieties of produce were for every liking. There was milk and meat (not always beautiful), fruits and lentils. Life of many steps were slow, casual, if pressed when necessary. Rocks became smooth under constantly moving water and the sun prepared wood and shelter for other needs. This description could continue even on and, if the carrying communities of those choosing to live together were examined, man lived as he could with a suggestion of spiritual care. Stability of faith in nature gave a promise of constancy. These words are

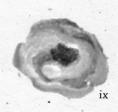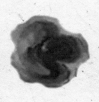

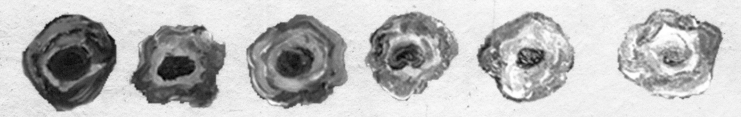

known, in writing (literature) as the "Pastoral Tradition," with nature, our Eden, God, our center, into the Medieval Period or the "Dark Ages;" no one questioned this principle. But the rigors of the thousand years of depression and loss of hope left people everywhere with questions; minds were troubled to the point of doubt and – voila – new directions were born. The renaissance and man became the center of the universe as in today.

What we refer to as the "Pastoral Tradition," came to know its undoing. The simple, the slow, the soft – it was, is familiar to working and sleeping routines, growth patterns, nutrition, birth and life as well as beauty and truth – the lovely all eventually fell to machines and factories in cities where people quickly forgot the rules of the natural, where flowers wept at the death of a poet, where none came to recognize the fragrance of rainfall on soil, where respect came to be shoved aside for a more convenient place.

Thinking and reasoning with or without physical activity can become a factor in fatigue which is difficult to relieve, but thinking and reasoning, especially on walks in natural settings or reading beautiful and wise words offer a fatigue which is easily overcome with benefits beside. Consider Browning's character, "Pippa": "God's in His heaven, all's right with the world." Nature gave a promise of stability, a constancy of faith. The factors of simplicity, strength, truth and wisdom (a box, a string, the thumb) are all positively reflected in the pastoral tradition.

A very prominent Russian writer, L. Tolstoy, who lived and wrote during the Crimean War, recorded the war, working long and with great effort on this pieces; it is one of the world's classics entitled _War and Peace_. He is also very well known for one of the world's greatest treatises on death ("The Death of Ivan Illich"). In his study during this time, pressed with work, he became aware of a Trinity representation of the natural, as "things" had used to be. He looked out his office window to see an apple fall in its soft, ripe sound; he was suddenly aware of sunlight streaming through his window, above his desk, and finally, he heard above other sounds, the horse hooves in their rhythmic clatter on the cobblestones in the street. This pastoral scene restored him – from out the past.

In reviewing mythology and histories, and throughout record keeping, unusual – beautiful, fanciful, ancient animals have been described. They are present in the oldest cultures, towardward to the Medieval Period; even until today, such still are seen.

The white, horse-like animal is noted in antiquity, having a long, waving mane and tail, cloven hooves and a single, spiraled horn in the center of his head. The horn was to have been medicinal in its contents. Also, the description likens it to the white hart, and the unicorn was to have been gentle, kind, and pure, to succumb only to a virgin, finally coming to be Christ's presence on Earth.

Perhaps the most worthy and accomplished of the major English Romantic poets has been said to be John Keats. Beside his personal repertoire of admirable qualities, he is appreciated as a fine craftsman. He became tubercular as a young man while nursing his tubercular brother, and although he continued to write, and

   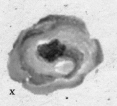  

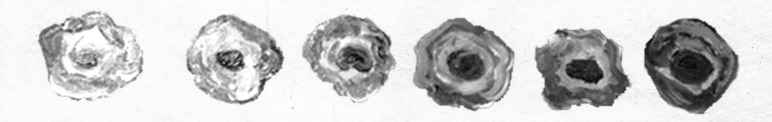

planned to marry his sweetheart, Fanny Brawne, he died at an early age, writing of holding beauty and truth, through death "Ode on a Grecian Urn," and "When I have fears that I may cease to be:" lovely, well-executed verses expressing his belief that beauty and truth are held for eternity, as that immortal, in accomplished works of art. "Endymion," "A thing of beauty is a joy forever; its loveliness increases: it will never pass into nothingness," and "Ode on a Grecian Urn," "Beauty is truth, truth, beauty; that is all you know on earth, and all you need to know –"

In sum, reviewing long years ago into recent times, truth and other voices including fables – indeed these still reflect the secret needs of a people and their origins. In our dreams and fancies lie our most pure motivational needs. They are, more often than not, mostly unknown to us: we are busy, always, with the day and its requirements. But the observing centras of consciousness, even when protecting itself, does, out of holy need, in selected given moments, become aware of its true requirements and motivations. In most truth, we wish peace and understanding. Such is not truly, completely possible to mortals – and so whatever the beginnings, the locale, the time period – we all look beyond what we know – for what we know is prescribed and dated. There is left the matter of beginnings and conclusion – the whispered words of "existence," "being," "death," "eternity," – and the growing questions to which we cannot find suitable answers. –Ah, thanksgiving for the respite of "long, long thoughts" which bring legend with historical record, to offer the draught.

Elizabeth

March 14, 2019

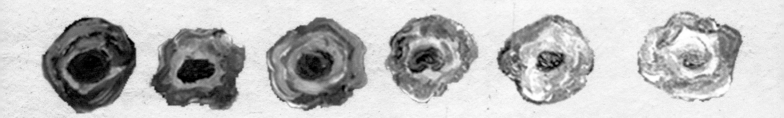

  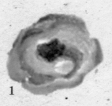 

  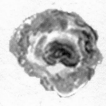  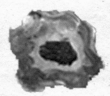 

His Noblesse

The grass pulled from the tender earth,

An ample draw of brilliant green;

And just beside, bunches of color infusion,

First shapes arranged in lovely form.

The small area beside the path became imbued

With the suns' turning wealth,

And the rolling sky about softened the gold,

Fragrancing the air.

The pale white, graceful being

Having just passed by,

Slowed his royal steps,

Paused a royal pause,

And returned to the ephemeral gift

He had only just stepped beyond –

Into his full noblesse,

And then onto his fully noblesse –

Laddened path – not with gold,

But with beauty in blissful solitude

And truth.

  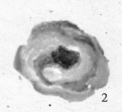   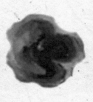

   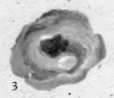 

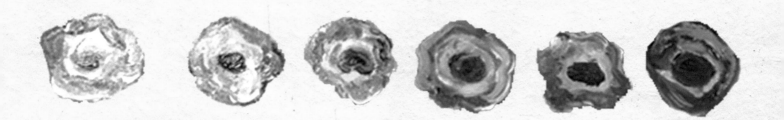

The Pause

Ah, hours in fancy,
Springtime's first:
My heart, a flower of fuchsia's hue,
Warmed by mid-day's
Streaming gold,
To give up a fragrance which,
With its petaled cup, hosting,
Causes the handsome,
Elite white hart, strong in his noblesse,
To pause and turn, just slightly,
In his stately gait,
Passing by.

Elizabeth
March 7, 2006
11:45am

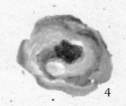

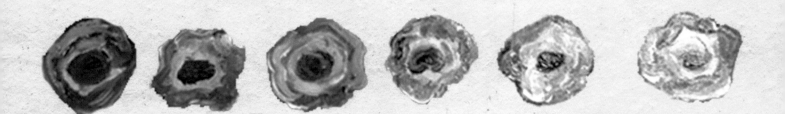

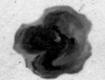  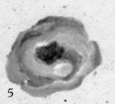 

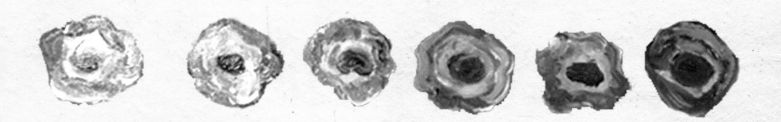

The maturing of my thought

Is both bold and tender,

As dear as gold,

As dark as death;

It does so Qustre in its

Various and divergent epiphanies,

Grieving me, unsettling,

More,

My already weary soul.

Elizabeth

April 15, 2006

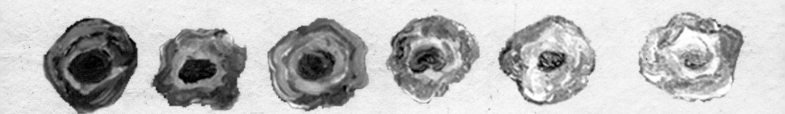

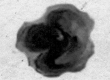  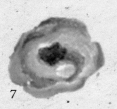 

  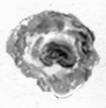   

Falling leaves,

Reminiscent of the pattern in a pretty dress,

And late, suggestive sighs of summer;

Straw collecting,

A wide rug of long stitches;

And the grapevine giving up its leaves,

In lessening light,

Yet to bare its golden treasure:

The mystique of autumn

Settles over father and son,

Fruit and herb,

The distant gold,

And melodies that enter

The beautiful tapestry.

Soon, coffee colors will have spilled

About the finishing green,

And that so new and full

Will lie under summer sighs.

Elizabeth

  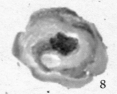  

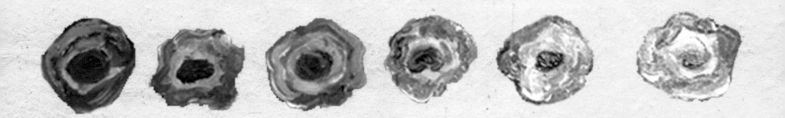

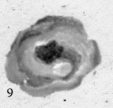

To my waking,

To my awareness,

Came a glory;

Light journeyed to flesh-like tones,

Growing quietly between the winter bare

But leaf gathering trees,

Much as the drape falling,

But into beautiful contours of clever, graceful lines:

suggested radiant flesh of a woman,

Still and waiting.

Such beauty is a gift that our thought

Can grasp, and hold,

And in the taking, know the true beauty

Of grace in salvation:

Ever God, in us.

Elizabeth

March 15, 2006

For Toni

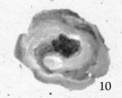

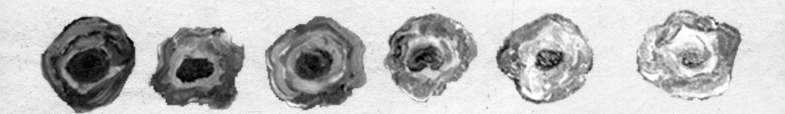

  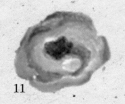 

Quiet came

Almost as an absence,

A knowing awareness;

Light fell at a distance,

As that forgotten,

And all else is a wanting.

The hurt is gone,

And its housing empty;

There is, in the balance,

Nothing.

All sound is asleep,

And laughter falls about in summers passed;

The afternoon is like a stone

Inside a shadow,

Passing over days of warmth;

A shell empty of its meat

And fullest flavor.

Elizabeth

  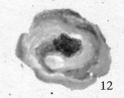  

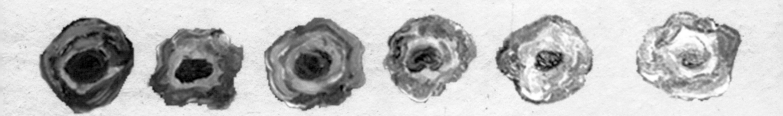

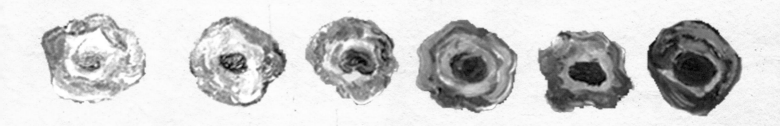

Sleep,

Is sweetest in the closing

Hours of the night,

When the fan of dawn begins to open,

And spreads slowly over mountains

Onto trees and meadows,

To touch the swan,

Patient in her circles and sittings;

For the darkest hours have passed,

And rogues and highwaymen

Must draw their cloaks

And run to their hiding places.

Elizabeth

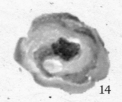

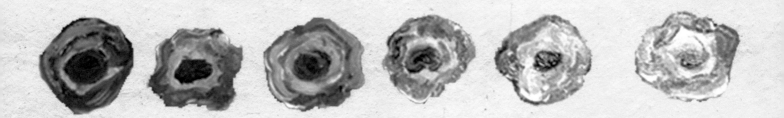

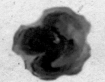    

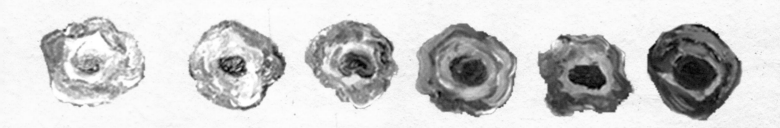

In the sleeping glow of the finishing moonrise,

In the smooth rock of flowing water;

In the coming wealth of the candle's charred wick,

In the canopy left of early morning's falling dew:

In these speak beautiful, poignant knowing in loss,

For in their emptiness fall

The lines of their late fullness,

Into shade and yesterday.

Elizabeth

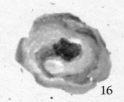

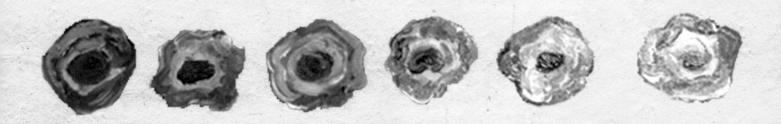

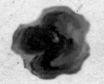     

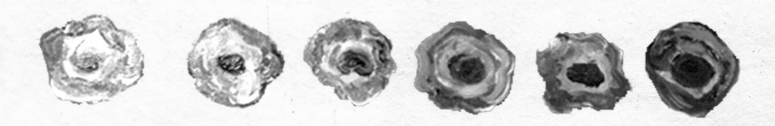

Somehow,

In time unmeasured,

The watermelon and vanilla hues

Of crepe myrtle have passed,

Replaced by crimson lying against

Bronze and gold,

Red satin and early morning yellow.

Is this not the way we pass from soft, sensuously

Tender colors into those deeper,

With more pigment?

But we stand under a sky

With less sun,

These colors leaning quickly

Into browns and farewells.

Elizabeth

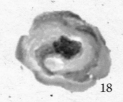

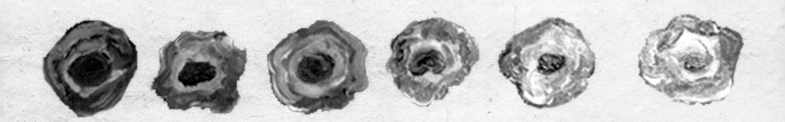

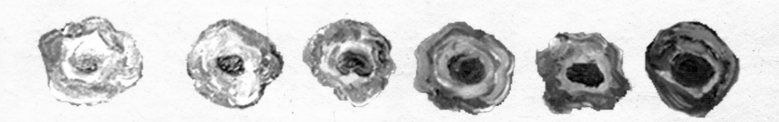

The spontaneous salutation,

Genuine, if perfunctory,

With a touch of freely cast sparkle –

A very burst of pleasant breath

Into a morning which

Had been before,

Only morning.

Elizabeth

March 7, 2006

  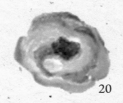  

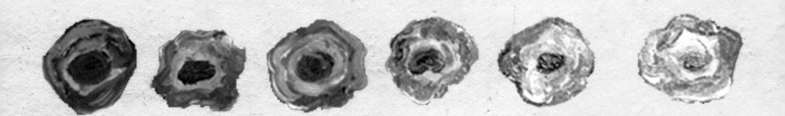

The weeping fig,

The laughing daisy –

Consented caverns from Freud's couch;

The contradiction of winter

And fading shadows rendering impotent

The blade of new grief.

We are none so wise ought but that

We go the long way home,

The long way of hurt,

And dark, and hope.

Elizabeth

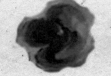

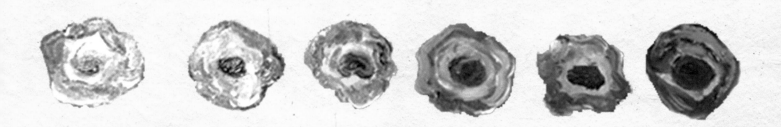

To look into the morning-glory's

Intimate blue,

To find the heart of the rose,

To catch the smile of the lily,

Altogether is to know beauty

Unto perfection.

We can sit in etudes soft within

The fragrant sea of warm gardenia,

But always knowing to learn

With passion and haste;

For their truth is as smoke in utterance,

Whispers lifting from the odysseyed earth,

Into our nostrils and invading our breath.

Elizabeth

  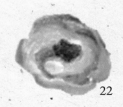  

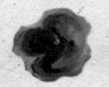  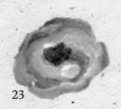  

23

  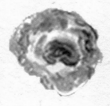   

All of our shouts,

Our murmurings are but begging compositions,

That we be recognized in our spirits,

That the moonfire anoint us,

That the day's star embolden us,

That we be known.

We wish most of all,

That we be known,

So that we may be joined to our beginning part.

Of it all, there is but a journey of days

That becomes in their fullness,

The richly tinted,

A lily in a photograph,

The word speaking silently from its page.

Elizabeth

-this record, a small benediction that forgives the day

  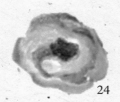  

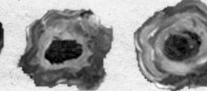
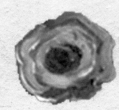
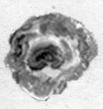

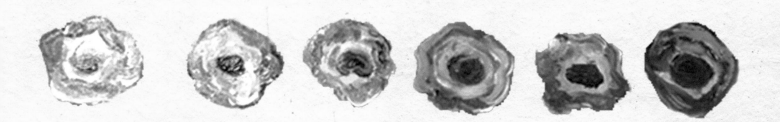

Spirit is all around me, everywhere –

Like Christmas sunlight,

As close as sentiment in memory,

Sounding like falling leaves.

I stand in it, touched by a good,

With a reverence for its grace,

Its windmill constancy–

Wearing its wealth promises

Resolution.

Elizabeth

  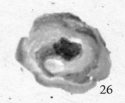  

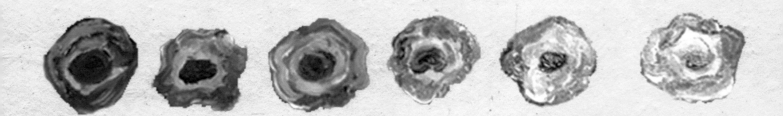

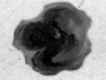  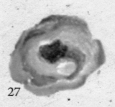 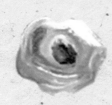 

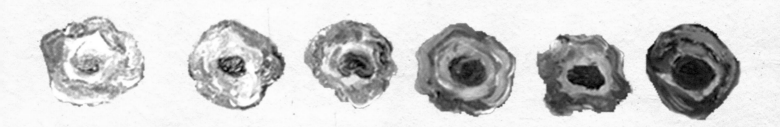

Whether we be holy men,

Monarchs, or street urchins,

Half of what we are is in

The reading of the script,

The applause that holds us up,

The light that forms our shadow.

We are not our own,

Only in beginning and concluding,

Only in our breath into the mortal,

And our breath unto that immortal.

Elizabeth

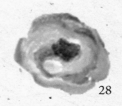

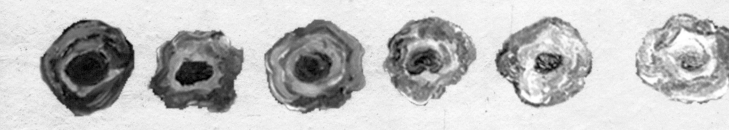

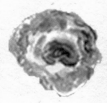

The Assuaging

I cannot save out a day from doomsday,

Except, perhaps, moments following a sunset,

Or an ave sung;

And touching are the seasons' progressions,

Casting a shadowed look behind and before,

Fears allying with irritability and longing,

Drawn by a winged creature of fancy –

These fatigue me and I arrive nearer the winter,

Forming an image that touches

With dark, flowering wisdom,

Inviting gentle reflection that finds

A world assuaging sorrow,

Of yesterday's summer warmth and ripe blackberry.

Elizabeth

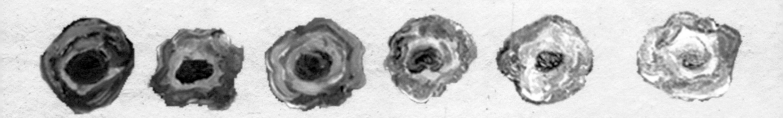

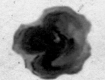  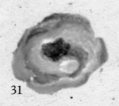  

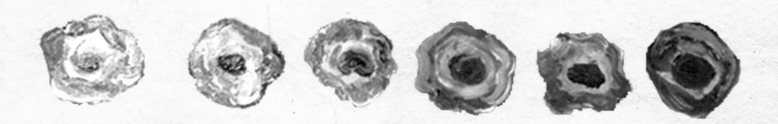

Cereal and milk in the night's three o'clock:

My lighted room throws shadows on a world

That is suddenly small and unfamiliar,

Except that within the nest of light

Where I have knowledge –

Knowledge that lets me know a surreal quiet and still,

With a presence heavy and sad.

I imagine that the world outside looks in,

And I weave a grand net of encounters;

I sit, a jeweled stone sewn onto a dark velvet,

Seen of all, and of all,

None.

Elizabeth

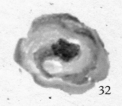

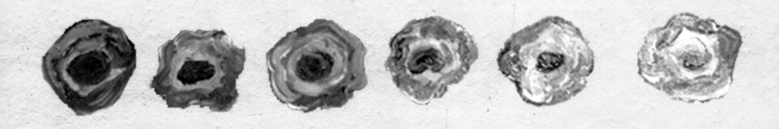

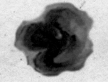     

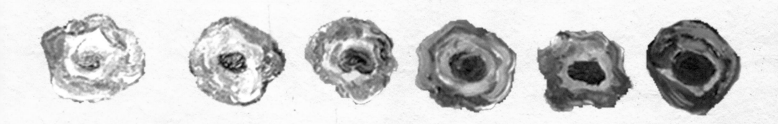

Return

The swelling of the organ

Lifts up the petaled smile of the gardenia,

And birds hasten when we walk;

These each become quiet,

For they are a reality only in moments

Of their recognition.

But like a ship come to port

From seas distant and wide,

Bringing treasures we do not now know,

The well of our thought allows the days

To come again, bringing gifts,

Even the fragrant nature of the gardenia.

Elizabeth

  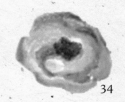  

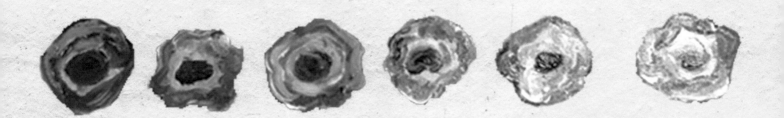

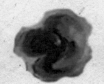   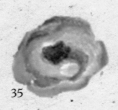  

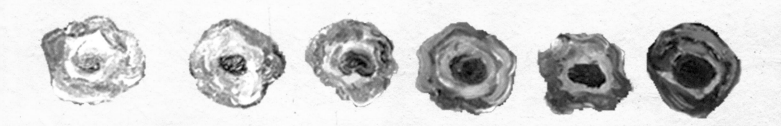

To go,

She picked up her things about,

Her gold, dear,

And in her gold lay her spirit;

It shown more than the visit,

And the sentiments in her last farewells.

Others within gathered up also,

But some knew of their gold,

Its passing quality.

And their sentiments were more true.

Ah, we need recital that we may be instructed.

Elizabeth

  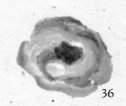  

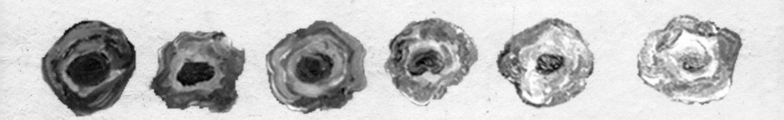

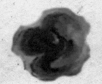    

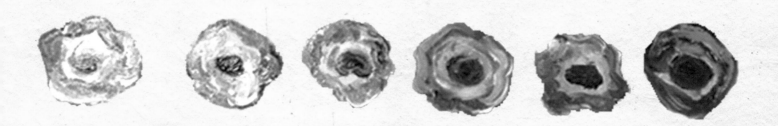

Moments of stillness brought a lovely melody,

To the accompaniment of thunder

And thousands of leaves out of the hands of autumn rain;

Summer blossoms wander in the wind,

In search of their lord of gold,

Anticipating the presence of cold,

And winter's grey sleep

-beside capturing our thought is quiet reflection;

Yet, reminding smoke, shadows and sighs,

And our hearts pull a bright silk over our deepest thoughts,

Those that struggle and fall, bitter lamentations.

Elizabeth

  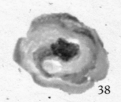  

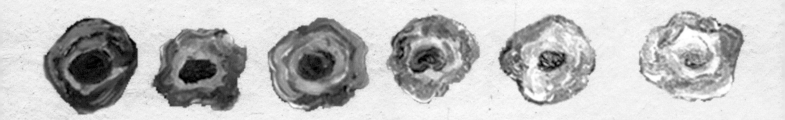

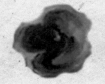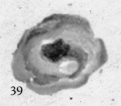

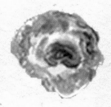

My moods,

Inside working circumstances,

Pull out of me,

In intense portions,

Blood and sinew,

Breath and will.

Lions tonight,

Walking on the beach,

In *darkened* moonlight.

Elizabeth

April 11, 2006

"Lions…" -a reference to Hemingway's

<u>The Old Man and the Sea</u>

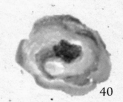

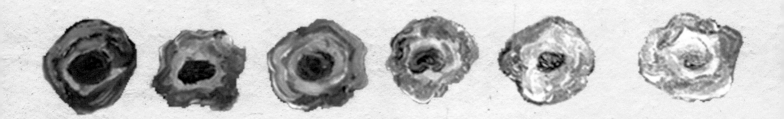

  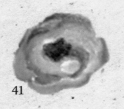  

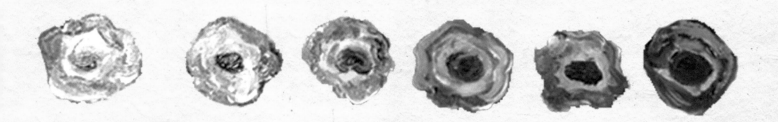

The image of the lovely pomegranate

And pear, together –

In their seasons come to the fullest ripeness,

These dressing my resting thought.

Elizabeth

May 6, 2006

Summer love, many times over_

  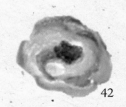  

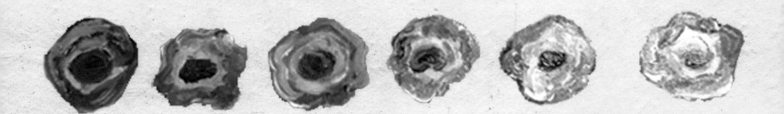

Can it matter that passing,

Like a pattern in a fabric rising out,

And receding into the background,

Is the only constancy:

Giving up joy, with grief,

Regret, and content out fatigue,

Yet, despair —

To arrive at acceptance.

Elizabeth

April 15, 2006

 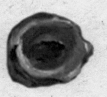  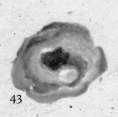 

  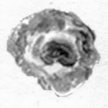   

My heart, my heart,

Close to deliverance;

No triumph –

A modest glory,

A small exultation?

Elizabeth

April, 15, 2006

  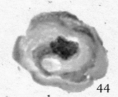  

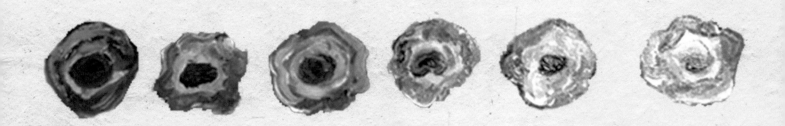

  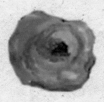  

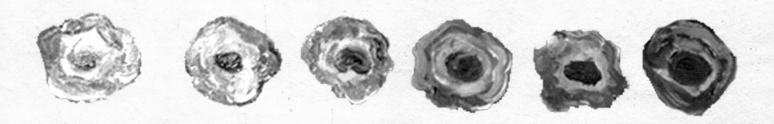

No score played out,

No verse read,

But, with their exquisite natures,

Leave me pale and small;

Wonderful stories flowing out of record

And wisdoms rising from

Revered volumes

Hold up to me my great lacking,

My unworthiness.

And were it not the lesson of the leaf,

The flower, the raindrop,

And our common grave,

I would, indeed, despair.

Elizabeth

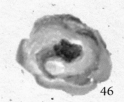

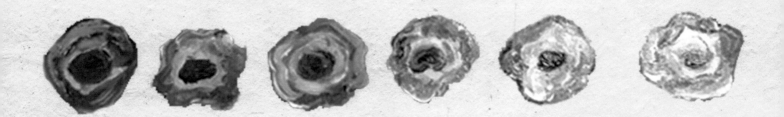

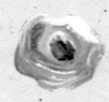

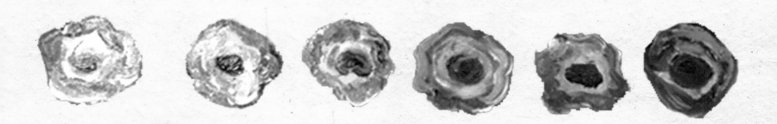

Perhaps the sweet pain in wishing,

Hoping, grasping –

Is more to be enjoyed than the

Consummation of these efforts;

For whether of an hour or a day,

There is the awaking, to be without,

And the quest begins anew,

The ravished rosebud never to be again

The color, the fragrance that

At first was its presence.

Elizabeth

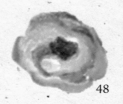

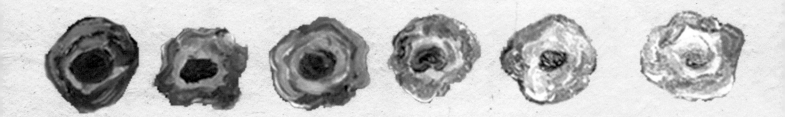

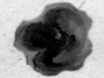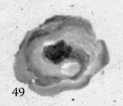

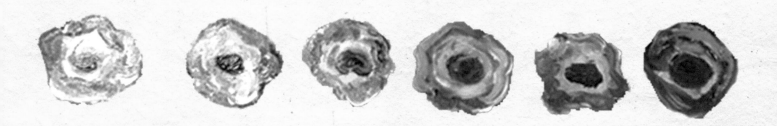

A heavy loneliness

Has settled on me,

In the music, the clay,

The silence of the night's darkness.

I know a becoming, far away,

And that I should see more of it before I become afraid.

Will there be another Camelot?

Another thousand days?

More, perhaps, the grey smoke

Of empty hours and memories that are,

In their insistence, unkind.

Elizabeth

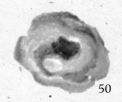

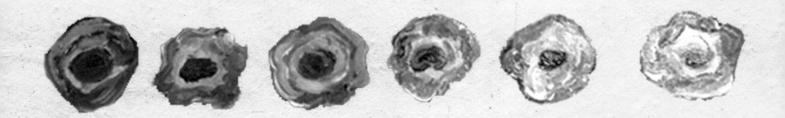

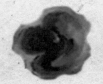   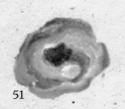  

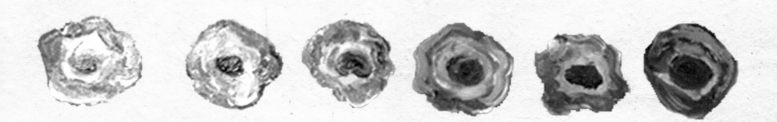

When we are gathering ourselves in,

Knowing the leaf and flower,

The sunset and rainfall,

Yet the smiles that linger,

And the touch which still burns,

We are then warm, filled,

Even with the shadowed,

Knowing that we have in the gathering –

Our joy in bitter sweetness.

Elizabeth

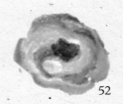

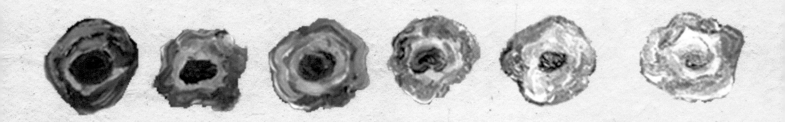

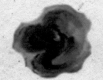  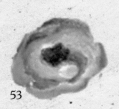  

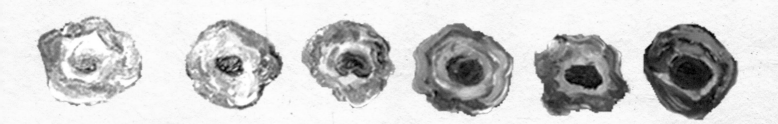

Images collect and fly away into the light,

Leaving broken lines and shadowed colors in the heart.

We know for only a little while,

A season abbreviated,

And we hold for even a less while.

Winter fills up knowing,

And summer is a sparkling jewel

That we keep in quiet places.

Elizabeth

Late 1990's – early 2000's

  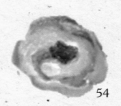  

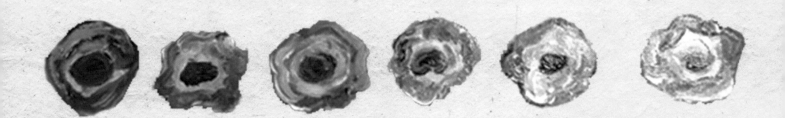

When our thoughts struggle

And our hands grasp;

When we weep in glorious harmony,

We stand taller than we are,

Becoming.

The very fancy we embrace.

Elizabeth

-late 1990's – early 2000's

Found this week, late March, 2006,

Six to eight hundred verses, quotes, forgotten.

In them are "little songs," and so I will record them

And not wait the new muse.

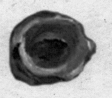

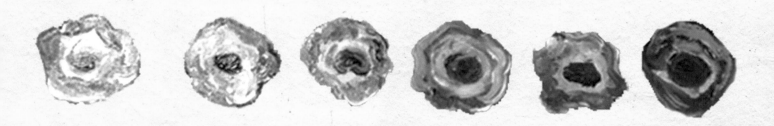

Notes attending the smallest sentiment

Before, just before:

-at day break, 6:30am,

Nearly full light, ivory under shadow

That will lift away in the innocent beauty

Of expectant sunrise –

Property only of Southern Springs, Mississippi, particularly –

More, to listen to the faraway loveliness;

Of the entering mourning dove:

Oh, my heart, can fullness know

All of inside to fill up the greater scape

Of all otherness.

Elizabeth

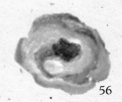

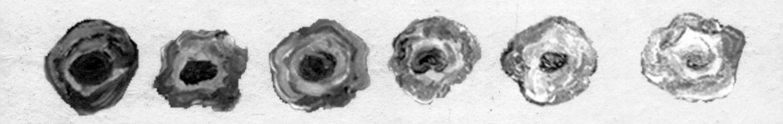

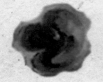  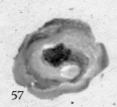 

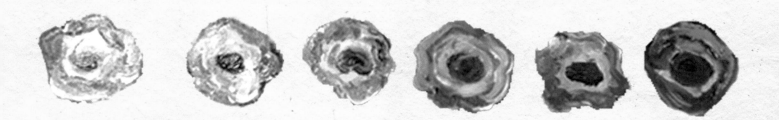

All at once the day was,

Be, is,

No matter its debutant colors;

It has come,

The golden carriage of hope,

Purpose, joy,

With the backward look

To yesterday's poignancy,

Tomorrow's purse of ample fare.

Elizabeth

March 28, 2006

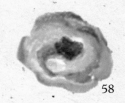

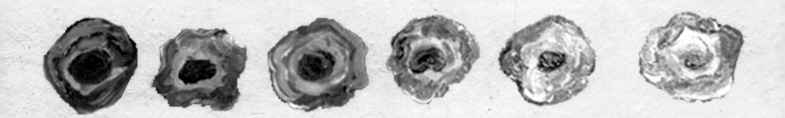

   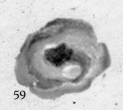  

  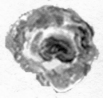   

First things,

Small graces, blessings

Of the deepest good:

Spontaneous thought,

To stand purposefully,

Blooming the lamps,

Touching candles,

Enlarging their fragrances;

Visiting among pieces,

Just so placed, to allow them now to become,

In their familiarity, old friends –

And then, the recognition of the porte,

The lock, the key,

The ritual of opening today,

To being, again,

Once more, again!

Thanks be to God!

Elizabeth

March 8, 2006, 11:45am

A good, productive morning – feeling well again –

  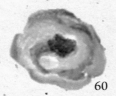  

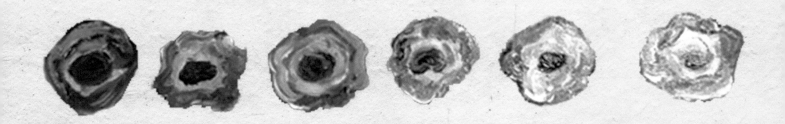

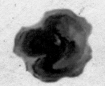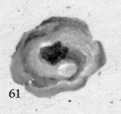

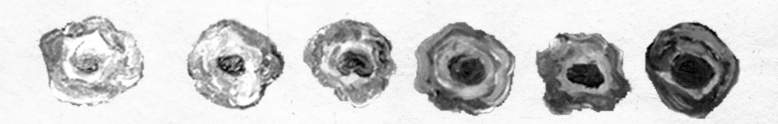

Music in darkness,

Thoughts wandering the halls

Of yesterday;

How sweet can moments be,

How much a harbor the chambers

Of the heart.

Elizabeth

March 8, 2006

Deep night, 1:40am

  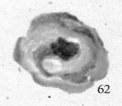  

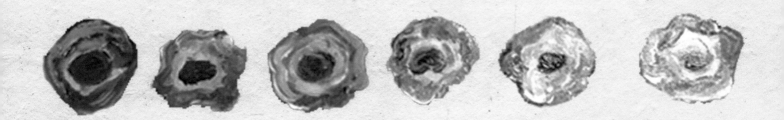

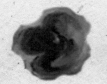     

I among roses and greens,

Very thousands,

Thee among my thoughts,

Many and more,

We within the spring sunlight

Of God's grace,

He blessing all with seasons

Of joy and hope,

Flourishing and harvest,

And rest in patience for yet,

Still, more gold.

How good is God that He does not

Weary to give us a first,

A beginning, to walk through

In gifting and taking,

Toward a balance of peace?

Elizabeth

March 7, 2006

Twilight, 6:15pm

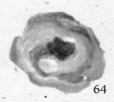

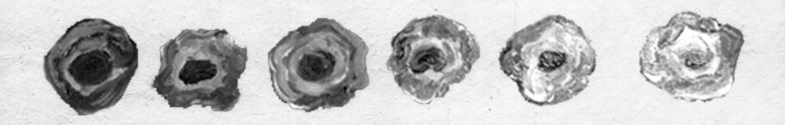

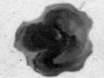  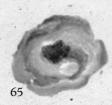 

There is, in each, us all,

A nature that points out, as an eager, rising mist,

To the larger natural;

In falling sunlight,

My thought was confirmed thus,

For I saw, through my kitchen window,

A small, black butterfly,

Winging about the brilliantly blooming

Hinot red azaleas-

A very kingdom in deepest hue and vibrancy –

In perfect peace of innocence,

Stillness and solitude.

As the rays continued their receding,

One, alone, caught the butterfly's anterior portion,

And I would declare that I could see a crown upon it,

I bowed under his fancied scepter,

More innocent in the moment,

The quiet, the stillness, the peace.

Elizabeth

March 7, 2006

evenfall

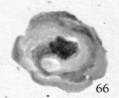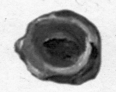

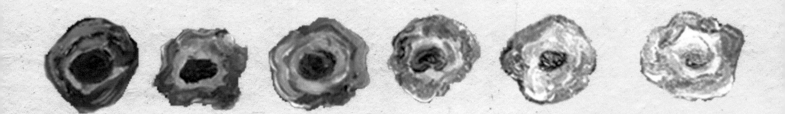

The cup,

So elegantly the hand graces,

In friendly,

Gentle ambiance.

Elizabeth

March 7, 2006

Noontime

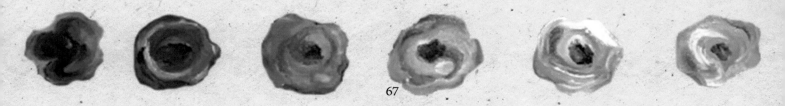

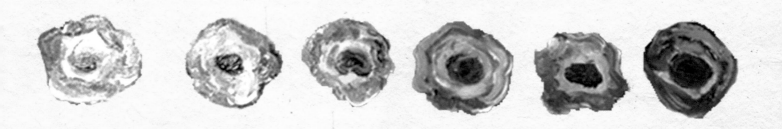

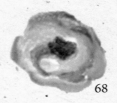

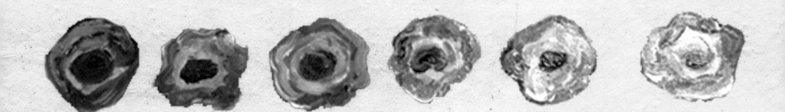

How lovely the bird

Against the sun;

How soft the fancied touch

Of wind among newest green;

How beautiful the thought

And its movement

In the heart.

Elizabeth

March 7, 2006

 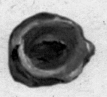  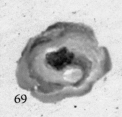 

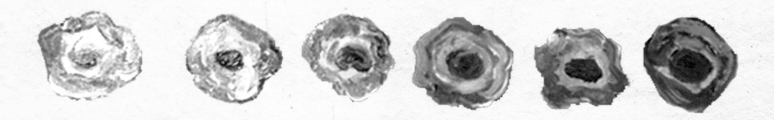

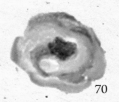

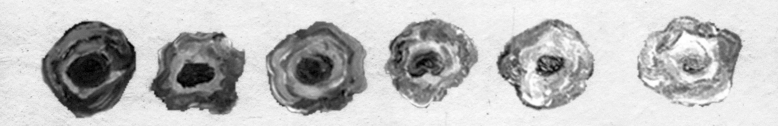

Behind sentiment

And the reason of sentiment,

Lies a whole knowing, complete.

Leaves past their vibrant colors,

Falling brown,

Pasteboard shapes,

Strew, in a dark mist,

The stored-away certainty

Of a new green.

Our mortal nature begs of us a reason,

A remembrance,

A commemorative melancholy

For the setting aside of numerous patterns,

Those beautiful, and noble,

In that their protest is quieted.

Could the shroud be sewed with

The thread of leaf green,

A needle of sunlight.

Elizabeth

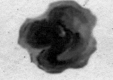

There were flowers

In their splendid robes

Since flowers dress appropriately for night;

Their fragrance holds heat,

And the dust of forgotten steps

Touches their colors,

Shining as a gently served, added brocade.

And so, the verse is one of night,

In early summer, when dogs

And butterflies accept dark,

And in the full quiet, curved rippling,

Furred muscles lie relaxed

And golden wings light up with innocent jewels,

In happy proclaiming.

In the dying of the day,

Nights echo each other more truly than do days,

And we are left to wander less, and find,

As we sit with ourselves,

The shampoo of peace

Grooms us for the morning.

Elizabeth

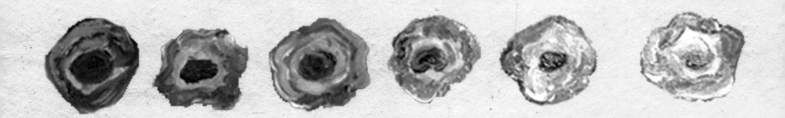

The Lost Verse

The images are faint,

As that hiding to the side of knowing;

Something of the moon occurs,

Her distance and personality

Of water and shadow

Without the gold of the sun.

The wind and trees enter,

For trees have presence in the night,

Wonderful fans that sweep the darkness,

With soft rushing sounds,

Not intense and foreboding,

But, with, all together,

Like walking toward home.

Elizabeth

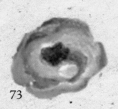

~ Elusive, still, gentle, innocently pure, the white hart has made his presence one of noblesse.
It is not a creature to hunt (sport) or even watch closely. All that is beautiful and good is
his kingdom – yet with bright spring flowers on his path, requiring a pause. ~

  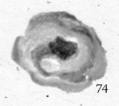  

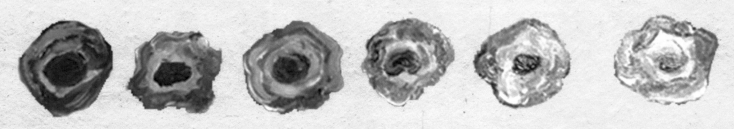

Conclusion

In considering the importance, the center of meaning of the word "pause," as used in the title of this work, and in the "title verse," a reference to the Arthurian Legends speaks well, fully. The incident which provokes the details providing a very worthy truth can be recounted: the "hesitation" to respond, of Sir Lancelot, King Arthur's most favored knight to Queen Guinevere, (she, dearest love to Sir Lancelot) and her last and very late request of the day, showed behavior in Lancelot requiring extended thought: more truth to balance action though antagonizing the queen, she then reacting to Lancelot's negative response by closeting her love, replying, "You hesitated."

Truth is an exercise in the balancing of factors working in given circumstances, revealing true motivations. To ponder and set aside time for viewing natural work of beauty and truth, equals wisdom in example.

When the complete festival of a holiday – religious, secular or, yet, the full unfolding of a natural season is finished, done – until the next time, we feel happy but experience some loss; yesterday and the present begin to take their places again, filled with forgiveness beside recollection. We are centered, for a short while, in our heart, sentiment bound, if passing, leaving the scourge, the pain of unresolved, but stirring dissonance.

The innocence in coming feeling is always kept, in some sweet fashion, but when shadowed, arriving by awareness through thought, its keeping is found in every echo, whisper, smile – yet all these images that can faster, suggest unhappy knowing. We struggle, then, always, with the truth of our most real sentiments and, with an effort approaching the persual of the grail, seek through our steps, our whole journeying, someone who knows intimate reality's truth; including our individual saga, to be enabled to know the glory of words that show understanding: sharing of pain, making possible, empathy and insights, to finally offer words, glances, gestures; the boon of comfort, out close, binding companionate care.

And so, in some part, into today's hours, recorded in the world's most esteemed, renowned literature, we give to innocence, the child, the idiot, the beast, the silently speaking natural, the unschooled – the simple – all that inside the tragedy in the latter days of Eden when innocence was given over in the coup of hubris for growing awareness. With growing awareness objective reality becomes more clear and demanding, the heart and sentiment acquiescing. And if in need, we may create (as recorded in thousands of years), the innocence of Eden once more, that we may be closer, briefly, to truth, if in some part fabricated – a myth, a fable, an achievable grail.

This circumstance is made possible by divine love's intervention into, our lives; whatever the particulars, the customs, the rules we come to acceptance of the intimately needing care that all sometime require: touched by a simple need, asking humble care, a glance of appreciation toward the upturned beauty of the unabled, nature's gift. Such (that of the flower and the beast) is our noblesse, in doing so; this quality we give to creatures of reality and fancy in its rare, select beauty and it will not fail in its execution.

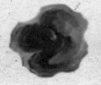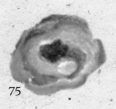

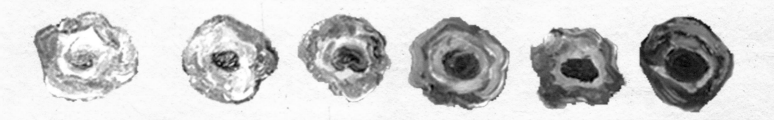

Elizabeth Afterthought

Since man placed his first step out of the realm of the "dark ages" and into that of a "rebirth," the "renaissance," philosophically, he established a weltanschauung with man at the center of the universe; the phenomenon, that of "self," has known no bounds; its time knowing boundaries have been set only by circumstances, spirituality being made a circumstance in itself.

It may be that the truism of extremes holds strong, even in giving attention to the self. As the ability to use our reason to observe and become ever more aware – of every entity we come to perceive – a veritable ever-growing constant; we court becoming fatigued with questioning, comparing, examining, evaluating – the entire process of knowing – so that as respite, we look for a simplicity, an innocence that is not ever requiring – and ironically, promoting peace: a flower's smiling hue, a bird's cheerful greeting, a child's humble love or a pet's unconditional devotion- these- beautiful truths that we only must recognize and accept. Myth and fable allow truth in the simple and true and require only the effort toward clear recognition.

For, yet, eons man has vacillated between two extremes of the obvious, in the yet innocent, not requiring credentials; and the obvious in the used and worn, often weary in observation, questioning and awareness (an awareness satisfied, at times, with the absurd). Perhaps myth and fable remain in all cultures, in all ages, all time, to balm those who lose, in efforts toward engagement, but hope, into surmising, to still continue with their dreams.

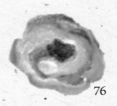

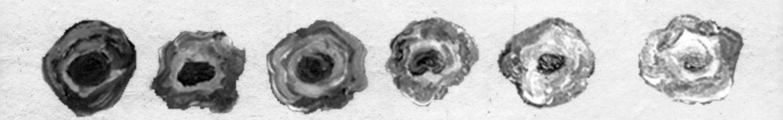

A Worded Rose

There is, in truth of innocence and purity,

a flowing out, like streaming moonlight,

whether in age,

such as the gathered softness of old world lace,

or the instant bright of a striking fire;

and left is never a shadow behind,

or needing absence,

nor an uncomfortable accounting

waiting before.

Elizabeth

May 12, 2019

Eventide of Mother's Day

   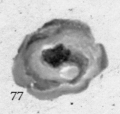  

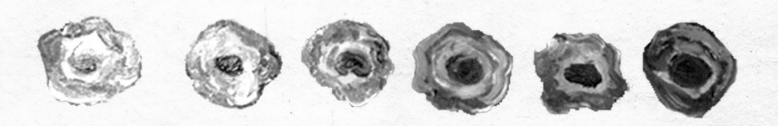

Edited by Hal

  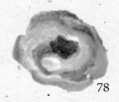  

   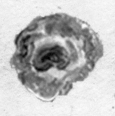  

Works by Elizabeth Clayton

I, Elizabeth	Shenandoah Songs	We Lesser Gods
2007	2012	2016
Songs from the Eleventh Month	The Sun and Geranium Poems	We Lesser Gods Addendum
2008	2012	2016
A Thousand White Gardenias	Scarlet Flow	In Springtime's Fields of Glory
2009	2012	2016 —
Unto Relationship	Seasonal Portions	Short Harvest
2009	2013	2017
Musings	The Myth of Being	Devotions in Elizabeth House
2009	2015	2017
La Libelule	The Quiet Sheba Trilogy	The Kept Ecclesia of Agatha Moi
2010	Three Volumes	2018
	2014-2016	
Chanson de Harold		
2011		

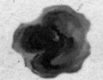   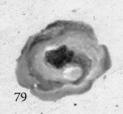  

  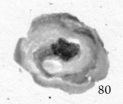  

Printed in the United States
By Bookmasters